Incredible IDIOMS

SONIA MEHTA

PUFFIN BOOKS

An imprint of Penguin Random House

PUFFIN BOOKS

USA | Canada | UK | Ireland | Australia
New Zealand | India | South Africa | China | Singapore

Puffin Books is part of the Penguin Random House group of companies
whose addresses can be found at global.penguinrandomhouse.com

Published by Penguin Random House India Pvt. Ltd
4th Floor, Capital Tower 1, MG Road,
Gurugram 122 002, Haryana, India

First published in Puffin Books by Penguin Random House India 2018

Text, design and illustrations copyright © Quadrum Solutions Pvt. Ltd 2018
Series copyright © Penguin Random House India 2018

ISBN 9780143444879

Design and layout by Quadrum Solutions Pvt. Ltd

Printed at Repro India Limited

www.penguin.co.in

Dear MOMS and DADS

Over the years, I have discovered that the smartest, most confident kids, are those who have great language and communication skills. They are able to get their thoughts and ideas across in the most effective way, and this helps build their confidence.

And one of the best ways to help them develop these skills, is to give them a strong foundation. We recognize that English is a language that will remain important to them in their future lives—both professional and personal. Which is why, in the **Fun with English** series of books, we have focussed on bringing alive those aspects of the language that will add flair to children's communication when they speak or write.

English is a language that has many subtle nuances. The simplest sentence can be brought alive with an appropriate idiom, a well-chosen figure of speech or a colourful proverb. The correct use of punctuation and phonic sounds adds dramatically to the written or spoken word. By focussing creatively on all these, the **Fun with English** series aims to help kids get comfortable with some of the more confusing aspects of the language in a manner that is exciting and challenging.

I've enjoyed writing these books and I've re-discovered the joy of English as I did. I hope you enjoy these books with your children too.

SONIA MEHTA

Hello KIDS

Have you ever wondered why English has so many strange and interesting words and phrases in it? What does the proverb 'a stitch in time saves nine' mean? What do you picture when you hear the idiomatic expression 'it's raining cats and dogs'? What's the difference between a comma and an ellipsis? These are just some of the many things the **Fun with English** series will help you find out more about.

What's more, when you're done with the series, you'll be able to use idioms, figures of speech, proverbs, punctuation and phonics like a pro!

Incredible Idioms

An idiom is a colourful and fun way of saying something. It is a group of words that have a meaning that is not exactly what the words indicate, but which communicate a thought or an idea.

When you say 'let's paint the town red', you don't mean that you will actually take a brush and paint the town with red paint! What the idiom really means is that you're going to have a lot of fun.

There are many different kinds of idioms. In this book, you'll see idioms based on

animals   clothes   food   colour   body parts

If you find yourself stuck at any point in this book, just remember that you can always use a dictionary or the Internet to help you find the answer, or just ask a grown-up. And of course, the answers to all the activities are there at the back of the book. So let's get right to it.

I hope you have fun with this book. I certainly had fun writing it.

Lots of love,

SONIA AUNTY

PS: Do e-mail me if you have anything you'd like to say about this book.

sonia.mehta@quadrumltd.com

Animal IDIOMS

There are many idioms that are to do with animals. Here's an example.

HAS THE CAT GOT YOUR TONGUE?

This doesn't mean that the cat has literally grabbed your tongue. It's just something people say when you take a long time to answer a question. It's a way of asking why you're not saying anything.

Here is an animal idiom list to get you started. There are many more to discover as you complete the activities on the following pages.

1. rat race — a way of life involving always competing with someone else
2. nest egg — an amount of money saved for the future
3. a fish out of water — to be uncomfortable in a new place or a new situation
4. to let the cat out of the bag — to give away a secret
5. a catnap — a quick nap
6. to hold one's horses — to wait a bit before saying or doing something
7. a bull in a china shop — a very clumsy person
8. a dark horse — someone with a surprising or hidden ability or skill
9. a cold fish — someone who seems unfriendly or unemotional
10. to stir up a hornets' nest — to create trouble
11. fat cat — a rich person with influence
12. clam up — be secretive about something
13. smell a rat — to feel that something is not right
14. to cry wolf — to raise a false alarm
15. pig-headed — stubborn

What's the Sense?

Look at these pictures. What idioms do they suggest? There's a hint with each.

These rats are trying to win a _____.

When you feel out of place, you feel like a _____.

When you reveal a secret you are _____.

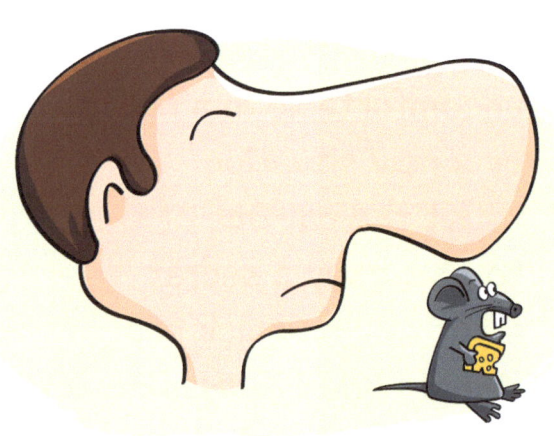

When something is not right, you _____.

Jumble Fumble

Here are some words that have been jumbled up. Can you unscramble them and fill in the blanks?

1 Mr Cautious was like his name—very cautious. He had saved a lot and built up a small _____ _____ `ETNS GEG` for the future.

2 Oh, boy! Greedy Pop can really eat. He _____ _____ `GIGDEP TUO` on pizza.

3 Pushy Bob has his eye on the best. He made a _____ `EBEILEN` for the best coat on the sale rack.

4 Funny Fran can't do anything original. She is such a _____. `PYCOACT`

5 Dozy Dan is always sleepy. He grabs a _____ `TCAPNA` at his desk at work every afternoon.

Crazy Crossword

Can you solve this crazy animal crossword?

DOWN

1 Miss Hustle-bustle is always as busy as a _____.

2 Hey! I told Charging Charlie to hold his _____ and not be so hasty.

4 Master Slow Coach walks at a _____'s pace.

ACROSS

2 Higgeldy and Piggeldy are always being silly. They love to _____ around together.

3 Chancy Charlotte makes the most of her chances. She manages to kill two _____ with one stone.

Wacky Word Search

Find the five animals hidden in this grid and then complete the sentences given below.

D	C	H	I	C	K	E	N	S	A
Q	Z	X	C	V	W	O	L	F	D
Q	W	E	R	B	N	L	K	J	H
W	E	C	L	A	M	W	E	R	F
A	S	D	C	V	B	B	U	L	L
S	H	E	E	P	R	F	V	B	G
Z	X	C	V	B	N	M	P	O	T
A	S	D	F	C	B	T	W	E	R
Q	A	Z	X	S	W	E	D	C	R

1 Mr Coward is so scared. He always _____ out of trying anything new.

2 Don't believe Lying Larry. He is always crying _____.

3 Oh, oh! Shy Sharon will _____ up if you ask her something.

4 Merry Martha is the black _____ of the Gloomy family.

5 Master Clumsy always knocks things over. He is a _____ in a china shop.

Tick Tock

Tick (✔) the right animal to complete each idiom.

1 Whiny Willie was a tell-tale and would _____ on his friends.

rat   goose

2 Sneaky Sam is a _____ burglar and really good at climbing up walls.

cat   bear

3 Miss Mumble, the class teacher, hit the _____ eye when she said that Tommy was the real culprit.

bull's   goat's

4 The Pickers family is as poor as church _____ .

mice   panda

5 Winky-wonk is such a trickster that he is always up to some _____ business.

monkey   cow

Idiom Bag

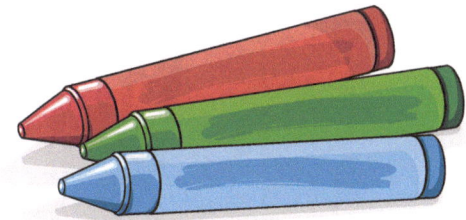

Match the idiom to its meaning by colouring both the idiom and its meaning using the same colour.

a dark horse

stubborn

snake in the grass

a made-up story

have better things to do

cock-and-bull story

be a cold fish

an unexpected winner

be very cold and unemotional

pig-headed

have bigger fish to fry

hidden enemy

Match Them Right . . .

Match the words in the two columns to make idioms. Then write each idiom below its meaning on the next page.

hold •   • as a bee

it's raining •   • in sheep's clothing

wild goose •   • chase

cry •   • one's horses

stir up •   • a hornets' nest

curiosity •   • killed the cat

busy •   • crocodile tears

be a wolf •   • cats and dogs

... Write Them Out

1 be patient

_____

2 heavy downpour

_____

3 someone with a surprising or hidden ability or skill

_____

4 getting too curious can harm you

_____

5 being very, very busy

_____

6 pretend to be hurt and weep

_____

7 create trouble

_____

8 pretending to be good while being evil

_____

Animal Farm

Choose the right animal to complete the idiom.

1. fat _____ : someone with a lot of money and influence

2. night _____ : someone who stays awake at night

3. lazy _____ : a lazy person

4. busy _____ : someone who's always busy

5. _____-eyed : someone with sharp eyes

6. _____ love : first love when someone is very young

7. the _____'s share : the biggest portion

Food IDIOMS

There are many idioms that are to do with food. When you say, **HE IS REALLY BUTTERING UP HIS TEACHER** you don't mean that he is actually spreading butter all over his teacher. You mean that he is flattering his teacher to get on her good side.

Here are some food idioms to get you started. There are many more you will learn as you do the activities!

1. a tough nut to crack — a difficult person to please
2. cake walk — something very easy
3. not everyone's cup of tea — not to every person's liking
4. couch potato — a very lazy person
5. full of beans — someone full of energy
6. to upset the apple cart — to create problems when there aren't any
7. to swallow a bitter pill — to accept something unpleasant
8. to eat humble pie — to accept a mistake
9. small potatoes — someone not very important
10. salt of the earth — a simple and good-hearted person
11. take the cake — being extremely silly
12. spill the beans — let out a secret
13. to rub salt on their wounds — make someone feel even worse than they already are
14. half-baked — something incomplete
15. a piece of cake — something very easy to do

The Right Choice

Choose the right answer and write it in each blank.

1 Nosey Parker has a finger in every _____.

milk   pudding   pie   pizza

2 Smarty Pants said the exam wasn't hard at all. It was a

piece of _____.

biscuit   cake   sandwich   cookie

3 Dancing simply isn't Mr Clumsy's cup

of _____.

lemonade   coffee   soup   tea

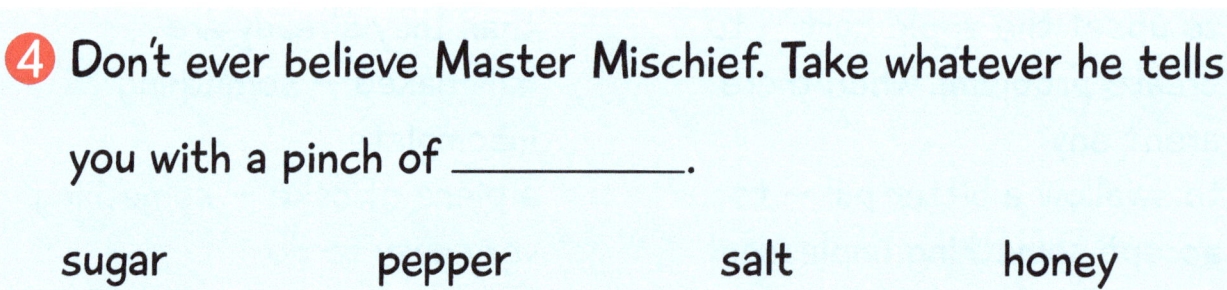

4 Don't ever believe Master Mischief. Take whatever he tells

you with a pinch of _____.

sugar   pepper   salt   honey

Foodie Grid

Complete the idiom by finding the missing word hidden in the word grid.

❶ Sloppy Joe is so lazy, he's a couch _____.

❷ The _____ on the cake for Miss Shop-a-lot was that she got a free hat with the dress.

❸ Master Stubborn is a real tough _____ to crack.

❹ Miss Forgetful forgot to take her exam. There's no use now crying over spilt _____.

❺ Miss Chatterbox is always full of _____.

❻ Mr Careless has put all his _____ in one basket.

❼ The hats Miss Flower has made sell like hot _____.

C	X	Z	B	E	A	N	S
P	O	T	A	T	O	N	M
V	B	N	N	E	G	G	S
A	Q	W	E	F	G	H	J
A	Z	I	C	I	N	G	M
N	U	T	X	C	V	B	N
Z	X	C	V	B	N	M	U
C	M	I	L	K	E	U	M
C	F	D	C	A	K	E	S

Match Them Right . . .

Match the words in the two columns to make idioms. Then write each idiom below its meaning on the next page.

upset •   • pill

half •   • pie

bitter •   • potatoes

eat humble •   • baked

small •   • of the earth

salt •   • the cake

take •   • the apple cart

 # Write Them Out

1 to spoil something for everyone

_____

2 something incomplete

_____

3 apologise and accept one's mistake

_____

4 something unpleasant and awful that one has to accept

_____

5 someone really honest and grounded

_____

6 be the best of the worst of something

_____

7 something insignificant or unimportant

_____

Yummy Crossword

Can you solve this crossword? It might just be a piece of cake.

DOWN

1 Gossipy Gimi can never keep a secret. He always spills the _____.

3 Ooh! Nice! That fire is making the room as warm as _____.

4 Oops! Too late. It's no use crying over spilt _____.

ACROSS

2 Selling newspapers is Honest Hugo's _____ and butter.

5 Nasty Nan is mean. She always rubs _____ in your wounds and makes you feel terrible.

Jumble Fumble

Here are some jumbled up words. Can you unscramble the words and write the right food item in the blanks?

1 Chancy Charlotte isn't interested in being a secretary. She has bigger _____ **IFHS** to fry.

2 Tweedle-dee and Tweedle-dum may be twins, but they are as alike as chalk and _____. **EEECSH**

3 Chatty Cho talks too much. His careless words always get him in a _____. **LEPIKC**

4 Nothing seems to hurt Tall Timmy. He really is a tough _____. **ICOKOE**

5 Mr Stuffy the principal is very strict. When you talk to him, it's like walking on _____ **GEG** shells. That's how careful you have to be.

Tick Tock

Tick (✔) the right food item so that the sentences make sense.

1 Terry and Cherry are so alike. They are like two  in a pod.

2 Smart Sam has many, many friends. He doesn't like to put all his  in one basket.

3 The tickets to the new movie sold like hot  .

4 To tell you the story in a   shell, Jumping Jenny won the race.

5 Tippy, Toppy, Teppy and Tappy all tried to write the essay together. It was awful. They didn't know that too many cooks spoil the  .

Body Part IDIOMS

Did you know that there are many idioms that are based on parts of the human body? For instance, you must have heard someone say,

OH SHE'S JUST PULLING YOUR LEG!

That doesn't mean that someone is actually yanking your leg off. It simply means that someone is making a joke or pretending that something is true when it isn't.

Here are some body part idioms that you may have heard of. You'll discover some more as you get going on the activities.

1. to get cold feet — to become nervous
2. to have one's head in the clouds — to be a day dreamer
3. to keep one's chin up — to be brave
4. to pull someone's leg — to lay a trick on someone
5. to let one's hair down — to relax
6. to play it by ear — to be spontaneous, or go without a plan
7. butterflies in one's stomach — nervous
8. to have one's back to the wall — to be unable to get away
9. a skeleton in the closet — a secret you want to hide
10. foot in the mouth — make a blunder
11. a stiff upper lip — being strong when facing tough times
12. butterfingers — being very clumsy
13. a frog in your throat — to find it hard to speak because you are hoarse or coughing
14. to fall on deaf ears — to refuse to listen
15. to have a heart of gold — to be a kind and generous person

Body Grid

Find the names of six body parts in the word grid. Then fill in the blanks in the sentences below.

1. Dreamy Dodo always has his _____ in the clouds.

2. Brave Barbara keeps her _____ up even when she is feeling very low and sad.

3. Tricky Trish is always pulling someone's _____.

4. Helpful Harry is always willing to stick his _____ out to help someone.

5. Oh, do come! It'll be fun. A chance to let our _____ down.

6. Slippery Susie escaped by the skin of her _____.

W	H	M	P	D	S	W	Q
A	S	D	F	G	H	E	U
F	T	L	E	G	Y	R	Y
A	S	E	D	R	G	T	Y
C	B	V	B	H	E	A	D
W	E	R	T	Y	U	I	O
T	E	E	T	H	X	C	V
A	W	S	E	D	R	F	T
G	A	S	D	H	A	I	R
R	N	E	C	K	R	T	Y
C	V	C	H	I	N	R	T

Body Double

Which body part would you choose to make the correct idiom? Circle it.

1 Acting Ashley never practices. He always plays it by _____.

nose   throat   ear

2 Cute Candy loves cakes. She has a sweet _____.

tooth   tongue   throat

3 Tweedle-dee and Tweedle-dum are always quarrelling. They are forever at each others' _____.

necks   chests   throats

4 It rained so much, that Drippy Don was soaked to the _____.

leg   arm   bone

5 Nervous Ned has butterflies in his _____.

heart   lungs   stomach

Crazy Crossword

Solve this fun crossword using the clues given below.

DOWN

1 Runaway Robbie is stuck. The cops have caught him with his _____ to the wall.

3 Rude Ronnie is so unbearable; it's hard to _____ him.

4 That sad movie always brings a lump to my _____.

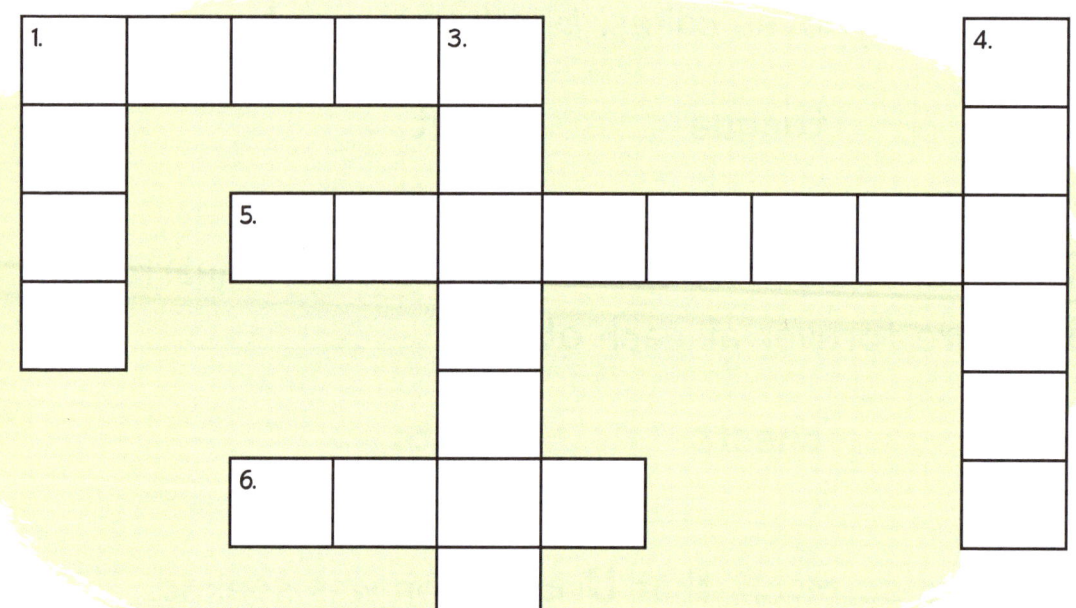

ACROSS

1 Suspicious Sally knows they are talking about her. She can feel it in her _____.

5 Helpful Harry is always willing to lend anyone his _____ to cry on.

6 Silly Sally is so irritating. She is quite a pain in the _____.

24

Jumble Fumble

Here are some jumbled up body parts. Can you unscramble them and place the right body part in the blanks?

1 Generous Joe is happy to give someone the shirt off his _____ AKCB .

2 Chimmy and Chammy both want to be first; it's a cut _____ HTRTOA contest between them.

3 Secretive Sara doesn't want the _____ SNOTELEKS in her closet to come out.

4 Master Rudesby ignores his friends by giving them the cold _____. REDLOUHS

5 Clumsy Carrie is always saying the wrong thing putting her _____ OTOF in her mouth.

Idiom Balloon

Match the idiom to its meaning by colouring both the idiom and its meaning using the same colour.

cold feet

look down your nose

break a leg

to be involved in everything

confess

get something off your chest

bite your lip

to be snobbish

a finger in every pie

hold back your comment

good-luck

to get nervous

Ticked Off!

Tick (✔) the right body part so that the sentences make sense.

1 Adventurous Andy had a hair/toe/chin-raising adventure.

2 When Snoopy Steven overheard what his friends said about him, his ears/fingers/eyes were burning.

3 The hall was so crowded, there was just no nose/elbow/shoulder room.

4 Brave Bob kept a stiff upper nose/lip/eyebrow when his team lost the game.

5 Jumpy Joe thought Pretty Pansy was lovely. He went weak at the jaw/knees/feet whenever he saw her.

6 Smart Alec has every line of the poem at the tips of his toes/thumbs/fingers.

Match Them Right . . .

Match the words in the two columns to make idioms. Then write each idiom below its meaning on the next page.

burn	one's feet
behind	are tied
drag	one's dead body
one's hands	one's spine
over	one's hair out
send shivers down	one's fingers
tear	one's back

.... Write Them Out

1 to suffer the result of one's actions

_____

2 to say something nasty about someone when they aren't present

_____

3 to go slow because one doesn't want to do something

_____

4 to be unable to do anything about a situation

_____

5 not if one can help it

_____

6 to find something creepy and scary

_____

7 to feel very frustrated

_____

Picture Search

Messy Mia has hidden the names of ten different body parts in her super messy room. Can you find them and fill in the blanks so that the sentences on the next page are complete?

1 Busy Betty's _____ are always full.

2 Clumsy Carrie really has butter_____.

3 Jumpy Joe can never settle down in one place. He has such itchy _____.

4 Nasty Ned gets his way with Timid Tommy by twisting his _____.

5 Poor little Timid Tommy is really under his mother's _____.

6 Wheezy Willie can't stop coughing. There seems to be a frog in his _____.

7 Stay alert everyone. We must keep our _____ to the ground.

8 Curious Carrie pokes her _____ into everyone's affairs.

9 The answer to the question is on the tip of my _____.

10 That was mean! Jealous Jenny stabbed her best friend in the _____.

Something's Wrong!

There's something wrong with these sentences. Can you replace the words in red so that each sentence makes sense?

1 The tickets are so expensive. They cost an eye and a finger.

_____

2 Weak Wendy has finally recovered. She is back on her head at last.

_____

3 Miss Stern, the class teacher, is very strict. The children's request for a picnic fell on deaf eyes.

_____

_____

4 That house is so lovely to look at. It really is a feast for the nose.

_____

5 Generous Gigi has a stomach of gold.

_____

Colour IDIOMS

Ever heard someone say,
LET'S PAINT THE TOWN RED?
Are you imagining them taking giant paintbrushes and painting the whole town a bright red colour?
That's not quite what the idiom means.
To paint the town red means to have a great time in town—go to restaurants, theatres and generally have loads of fun.

There are many idioms that are to do with colour. Here are some.
You'll find more in the activities on the following pages.

1. caught red-handed — caught in the act of doing something wrong
2. born with a silver spoon in one's mouth — born to a rich and privileged life
3. to see red — to get very angry
4. a white lie — a lie told to prevent someone being upset or hurt
5. to show one's true colours — to reveal one's real self
6. to blacklist — to disallow someone from doing something
7. blue-blooded — coming from a noble family
8. white elephant — an expensive object you can't rid of
9. red flag — a warning
10. grey cells — brain cells
11. flying colours — with great success
12. the pot calling the kettle black — criticizing someone for a fault they themselves have
13. blue-eyed boy — a favourite person
14. grey area — something that is unclear
15. roll out the red carpet — give someone a grand welcome

Colourful Word Grid

Can you find the names of seven colours in the grid below and use them to complete the sentences on the next page?

S	D	F	G	O	L	D	O	N	A
Q	W	E	R	T	Y	U	I	O	P
Q	B	L	A	C	K	R	T	Y	P
A	S	D	F	G	H	J	K	L	I
Y	U	K	D	B	L	U	E	J	N
R	Z	X	C	V	B	N	M	P	K
E	T	B	L	A	C	K	G	J	H
D	R	W	S	I	L	V	E	R	D
S	E	C	V	B	N	M	F	G	S
Q	W	W	H	I	T	E	C	V	P

1 Hermione struck a _____ mine when she found a pile of rare books.

2 Grumpy George sees _____ every time someone calls him grumpy.

3 Oh, wow! Out of the _____, Miss Thatch, the class teacher announced a picnic.

4 Hahaha! That was funny. Funny Fran is tickled _____.

5 Ouch! Nasty Ned hit Timid Tommy so hard that he gave him a _____ eye.

6 Kind Katie told a _____ lie to her friend when she wasn't selected for the play because she sang so badly.

7 Miss Markle got the job handed to her on a _____ platter.

Colour Hunt

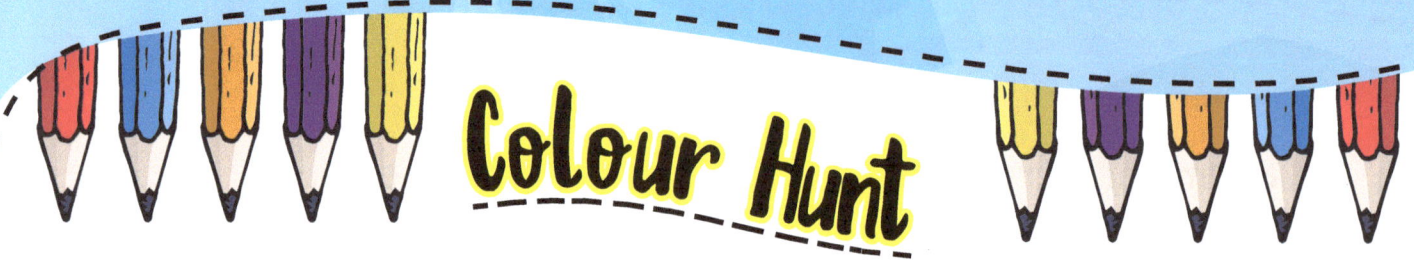

There are eight names of colours hidden in the colourful picture below. They all are a part of an idiom. Can you find them and write them in the correct blanks on the next page?

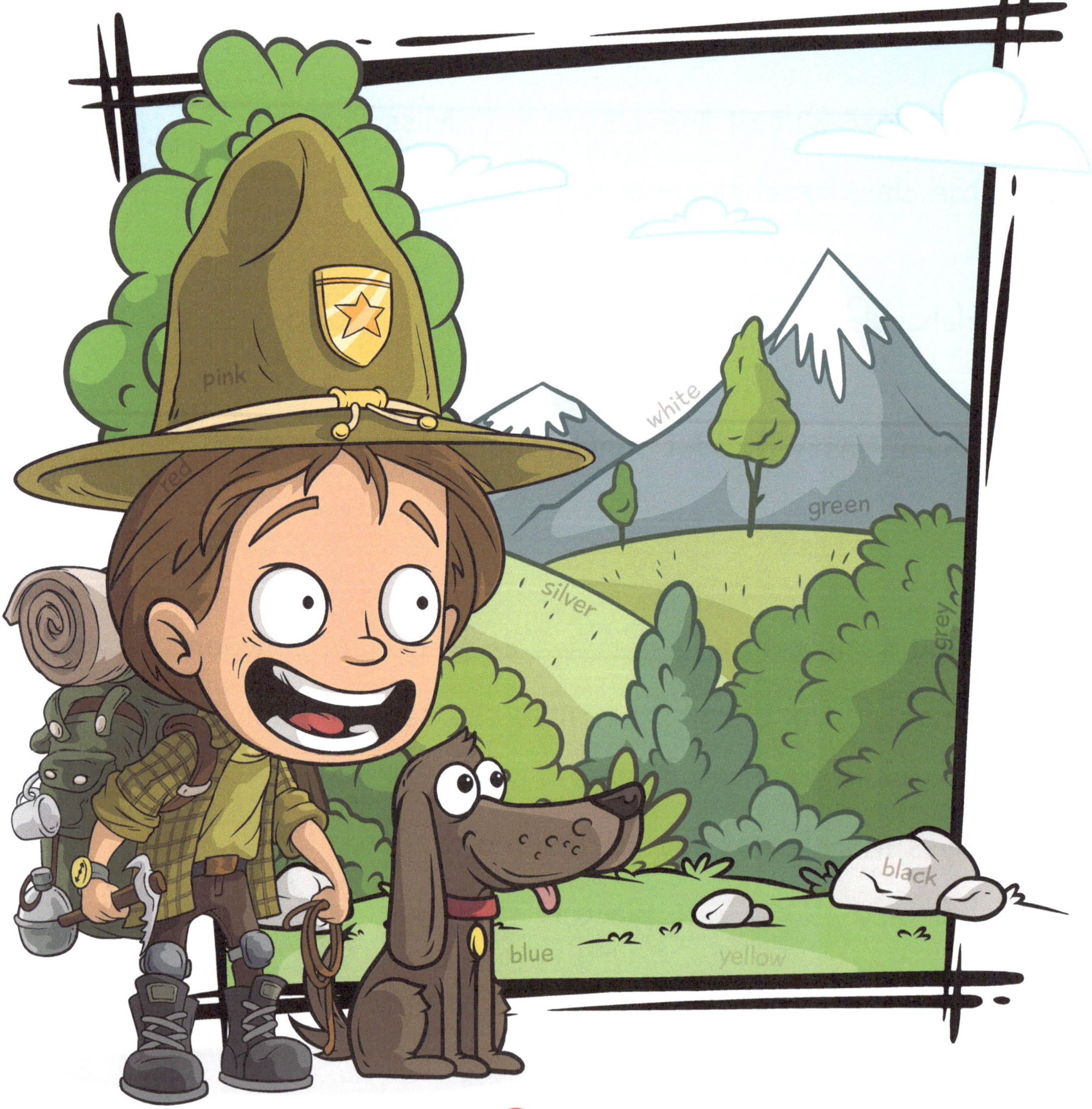
pink
white
red
green
silver
grey
black
blue
yellow

1 The school decided to _____list the children who disobeyed their teachers.

2 Princess Pippa is a real princess. She is a _____-blooded royal.

3 Yay! Our principal has given us the _____ signal to go ahead and plan the school trip.

4 Healthy Harry is always in the _____ of health.

5 Raging Ron sees _____ when anyone doesn't do as he asks.

6 Peace! Can't you see the opposite side has raised a _____ flag?

7 Smart Sally uses her _____ cells rather cleverly.

8 Richie Rich was born with a _____ spoon in his mouth.

Colourful Crossword

Solve this crossword and fill in the missing words.

ACROSS

1 Smart Sam passed the test with flying _____.

2 Quiet Queenie talks only once in a _____ moon.

3 Julia Starr is one of the finest actors of the _____ screen.

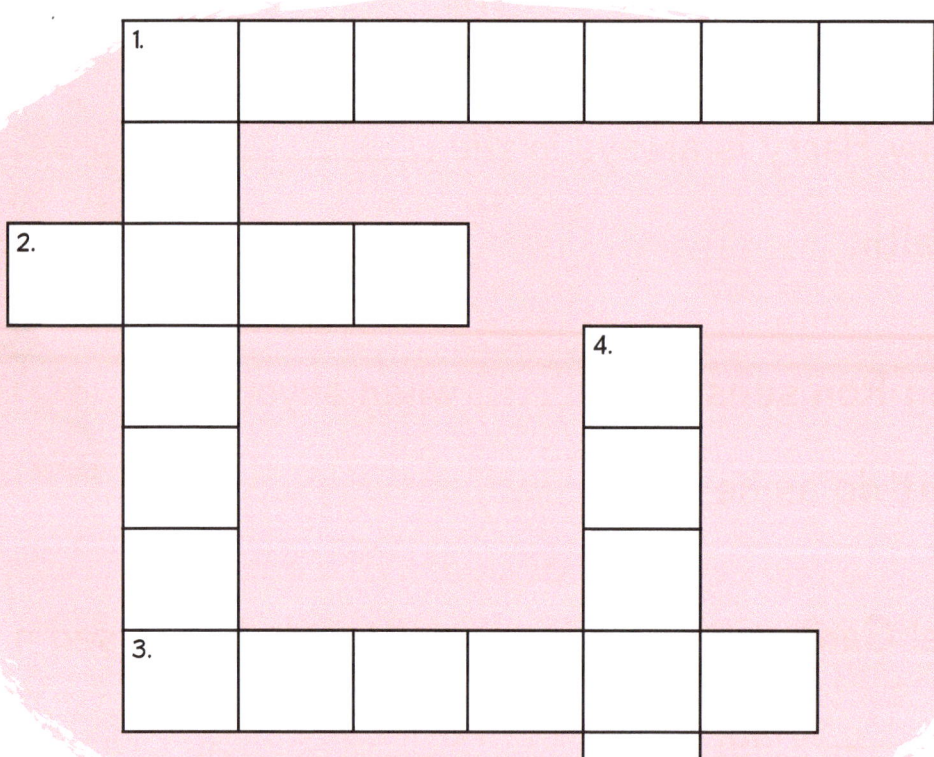

DOWN

1 Sneaky Sue showed her true _____ when she complained about her best friend.

4 Envious Ella went _____ with envy when she saw Jenny's new car.

Jumble Fumble

Here are some jumbled up names of colours. Can you unscramble them and put the right colours in the blanks?

1. Jealous Jenny calling Envious Ella a mean girl is like the pot calling the kettle _____. **KCLAB**

2. The school really rolled out the _____ **DRE** carpet for the chief guest.

3. Goody Garfield is the _____ **LEBU-** eyed boy of his class.

4. Hmmm! Whether the hen came first, or the egg is a _____ **RGYE** area.

5. Granny Gloria is in the _____ **KNPI** of health.

Clothes IDIOMS

I'm sure you must have heard a grown up say something like,

THAT DINNER WAS EXPENSIVE. IT BURNT A HOLE IN MY POCKET.

That doesn't mean that the dinner literally burnt a hole in their pocket? It is just another idiom that means the dinner was very, very expensive.

Here are some fun idioms based on clothes and other things we wear. You will discover more as you do the activities.

1. at the drop of a hat — happen instantly, without any delay
2. to hit below the belt — to be mean and unfair
3. roll up one's sleeves — get ready to work hard
4. to wear the pants in the family — to be the boss
5. laugh up one's sleeve — to laugh secretively
6. get the boot — be sacked from a job
7. old hat — old news
8. to hang up one's hat — to retire
9. line one's own pockets — to make some money
10. to burn a hole in one's pocket — to spend more than you can afford
11. handle someone with kid gloves — handle someone very gently
12. have ants in one's pants — be restless
13. lose one's shirt — to lose everything one has
14. have a card up one's sleeve — have a back-up plan
15. to roll up one's sleeves — to get ready for some work

Dress Up Grid

Can you find words related to clothes in the grid to complete the sentences that follow?

D	B	E	L	T	S	S	A
F	G	H	J	K	L	L	S
Q	G	C	A	P	J	K	L
S	H	O	E	S	H	J	E
A	F	F	D	F	G	N	E
X	C	L	O	D	K	N	V
Z	X	C	S	C	V	B	E
T	R	O	U	S	E	R	S

1 Thoughtful Thomas is trying to figure it out. He's put on his thinking _____.

2 Considerate Carrie always thinks about others, because she puts herself in their _____.

3 Hardworking Hans is ready to roll up his _____ and get to work.

4 Things are so expensive now that we must tighten our _____.

5 Mrs Bullpen wears the _____ in the family. Everyone has to obey her.

Match Them Right . . .

Match the words in the two columns to make idioms. Then write each idiom below its meaning on the next page.

burn a hole •   • in one's pants

handle someone •   • up one's sleeve

have ants •   • is on the other foot

lose •   • the boot

have a card •   • with kid gloves

the shoe •   • one's shirt

give someone •   • in my pocket

1 find something very expensive

_____

2 be very careful and gentle with someone

_____

3 be restless and always moving around

_____

4 get very angry

_____

5 have a secret plan

_____

6 the opposite is true

_____

7 fire someone from a job or kick someone out

_____

Idiom Tags

Match the idiom to its meaning by colouring both the idiom and its meaning using the same colour.

laugh up one's sleeve

get the boot

to leave a job after a long time

earn money in an illegal way

scare the pants off someone

to laugh quietly to oneself

old hat

to be fired from a job

hang up one's hat

some thing old and familiar

line one's own pockets

to frighten someone very badly

ANSWERS

Page 12 Animal Farm
1. fat cat   2. night owl   3. lazy pig   4. busy bee
5. eagle-eyed   6. puppy love   7. the lion's share

Page 14 The Right Choice
1. pie   2. cake   3. tea   4. salt

Page 15 Foodie Grid
1. POTATO   2. ICING   3. NUT   4. MILK   5. BEANS
6. EGGS   7. CAKES

C	X	Z	B	E	A	N	S
P	O	T	A	T	O	N	M
V	B	N	N	E	G	G	S
A	Q	W	E	F	G	H	J
A	Z	I	C	I	N	G	M
N	U	T	X	C	V	B	N
Z	X	C	V	B	N	M	U
C	M	I	L	K	E	U	M
C	F	D	C	A	K	E	S

Page 16 Match Them Right . . .
upset—the apple cart; half—baked; bitter—pill; eat humble—pie; small—potatoes; salt—of the earth; take—the cake

Page 17 . . . Write Them Out
1. upset the apple cart   2. half-baked   3. eat humble pie
4. bitter pill   5. salt of the earth   6. take the cake
7. small potatoes

Page 18 Yummy Crossword

			B		
B	R	E	A	D	
			A		
			N		
	T	S			
	O		M		
	A		I		
	S	A	L	T	
	T		K		

Page 19 Jumble Fumble
1. FISH   2. CHEESE   3. PICKLE   4. COOKIE   5. EGG

Page 20 Tick Tock
1. peas   2. eggs   3. cakes   4. nut   5. broth

Page 22 Body Grid

W	H	M	P	D	S	W	Q
A	S	D	F	G	H	E	U
F	T	L	E	G	Y	R	Y
A	S	E	D	R	G	T	Y
C	B	V	B	H	E	A	D
W	E	R	T	Y	U	I	O
T	E	E	T	H	X	C	V
A	W	S	E	D	R	F	T
G	A	S	D	H	A	I	T
R	N	E	C	K	R	T	Y
C	V	C	H	I	N	R	T

1. HEAD   2. CHIN   3. LEG   4. NECK   5. HAIR
6. TEETH

Page 23 Body Double
1. ear   2. tooth   3. throats   4. bones   5. stomach

Page 4 What's the Sense?
rat race, fish out of water, letting the cat out of the bag, smell a rat

Page 5 Jumble Fumble
1. NEST EGG   2. PIGGED OUT   3. BEELINE
4. COPYCAT   5. CATNAP

Page 6 Crazy Crossword

				B
H	O	R	S	E
	O			E
B	I	R	D	S
	S		N	
	E		A	
	S		I	
			L	

Page 7 Wacky Word Search

D	C	H	I	C	K	E	N	S	A
Q	Z	X	C	V	W	O	L	F	D
Q	W	E	R	B	N	L	K	J	H
W	E	C	L	A	M	W	E	R	F
A	S	D	C	V	B	B	U	L	L
S	H	E	E	P	R	F	V	B	G
Z	X	C	V	B	N	M	P	O	T
A	S	D	F	C	B	T	W	E	R
Q	A	Z	X	S	W	E	D	C	R

1. CHICKENS   2. WOLF   3. CLAM   4. SHEEP   5. BULL

Page 8 Tick Tock
1. rat   2. cat   3. bull's   4. mice   5. monkey

Page 9 Idiom Bag
a dark horse: an unexpected winner; pig-headed: stubborn; snake in the grass: hidden enemy; cock and bull story: a made-up story; have bigger fish to fry: have better things to do; be a cold fish: be very cold and unemotional

Page 10 Match Them Right . . .
hold—one's horses; it's raining—cats and dogs; wild goose—chase; cry—crocodile tears; stir up—a hornets' nest; curiosity—killed the cat; busy—as a bee; be a wolf—in sheep's clothing

Page 11 . . . Write Them Out
1. hold one's horses
2. it's raining cats and dogs
3. wild goose chase
4. curiosity killed the cat
5. busy as a bee
6. cry crocodile tears
7. stir up a hornets' nest
8. be a wolf in sheep's clothing

Page 24 Crazy Crossword

	¹B	O	N	E	³S			⁴T
	A				T			H
	²C		⁵S	H	O	U	L	D	E	R
	K				M			O
					A			A
		⁶N	E	C	K			T
					H			

Page 25 Jumble Fumble
1. BACK   2. THROAT   3. SKELETONS
4. SHOULDER   5. FOOT

Page 26 Idiom Balloon
cold feet: to get nervous; break a leg: good-luck; look down your nose: to be snobbish: get something off your chest: confess; bite your lip: hold back your comment; a finger in every pie: to be involved in everything;

Page 27 Ticked Off
1. hair   2. ears   3. elbow   4. lip   5. knees   6. fingers

Page 28 Match Them Right . . .
burn—one's fingers; behind—one's back; drag—one's feet; one's hands—are tied; over—one's dead body; send shivers down—one's spine; tear—one's hair out

Page 29 . . . Write Them Out
1. burn one's fingers   2. behind one's back   3. drag one's feet
4. one's hands are tied   5. over one's dead body
6. send shivers down one's spine   7. tear one's hair out

Page 30 – 31 Picture Search
1. HANDS   2. FINGERS   3. FEET   4. ARMS   5. THUMB
6. THROAT   7. EARS   8. NOSE   9. TONGUE   10. BACK

Page 32 Something's Wrong
1. The tickets are so expensive. They cost an arm and a leg.
2. Finally Weak Wendy has recovered. She is back on her head at last.
3. Miss Stern, the class teacher is very strict. The children's request for a picnic fell on deaf ears.
4. That house is so lovely to look at. It really is a feast for the eyes.
5. Generous Gigi has a heart of gold.

Page 34 Colourful Word Grid

1. GOLD   2. RED   3. BLUE   4. PINK   5. BLACK
6. WHITE   7. SILVER

Page 36–37 Colour Hunt
1. black   2. blue   3. green   4. pink   5. red   6. white   7. grey
8. silver

Page 38 Colourful Crossword

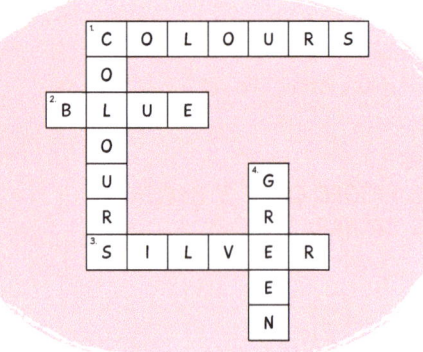

Page 39 Jumble Fumble
1. BLACK   2. RED   3. BLUE   4. GREY   5. PINK

Page 41 Dress up Grid

D	B	E	L	T	S	S	A
F	G	H	J	K	L	L	S
Q	G	C	A	P	J	K	L
S	H	O	E	S	H	J	E
A	F	F	D	F	G	N	E
X	C	L	O	D	K	N	V
Z	X	C	S	C	V	B	E
T	R	O	U	S	E	R	S

1. CAP   2. SHOES   3. SLEEVES   4. BELTS
5. TROUSERS

Page 42 Match Them Right . . .
burn a hole—in my pocket; handle someone—with kid gloves; have ants—in one's pants; lose—one's shirt; have a card—up one's sleeve; the shoe—is on the other foot; give someone—the boot

Page 43 . . . Write Them Out
1. burn a hole in my pocket
2. handle someone with kid gloves
3. have ants in one's pants
4. lose one's shirt
5. have a card up one's sleeve
6. the shoe is on the other foot
7. give someone the boot

Page 44 Idiom Tags
laugh up one's sleeve: to laugh quietly to oneself; get the boot: to be fired from a job; hang up one's hat: to leave a job after a long time; old hat: some thing old and familiar; scare the pants off someone: to frighten someone very badly; line one's own pockets: earn money in an illegal way